ZOMBIE HAIKU

Ryan Mecum

D0064243

HOW BOOKS Cincinnati, Ohio

www.howdesign.com

For more fine books from F+W Publications, visit www.fwbookstore.com.

12 11 10 09 08   5 4 3 2

Distributed in Canada by Fraser Direct, 100 Armstrong Avenue,
Georgetown, Ontario, Canada L7G 5S4, Tel: (905) 877-4411. Distributed
in the U.K. and Europe by David & Charles, Brunel House, Newton Abbot,
Devon, TQ12 4PU, England, Tel: (+44) 1626-323200, Fax: (+44) 1626-
323319, E-mail: postmaster@davidandcharles.co.uk. Distributed in
Australia by Capricorn Link, P.O. Box 704, Windsor, NSW 2756
Australia, Tel: (02) 4577-3555.

Library of Congress Cataloging-in-Publication Data

Mecum, Ryan.
  Zombie haiku / Ryan Mecum.
      p. cm.
  ISBN 978-1-60061-070-7 (pbk. : alk. paper)
 1. Haiku--Humor. 2. Zombies--Humor. I. Title.
  PN6231.H28M43 2008
  818'.602--dc22

                                        2008008678

Editor: Amy Schell
HOW Books Art Director: Grace Ring
Production Coordinator: Greg Nock
Photographer: Ryan Mecum

curio
press

Designer/Packager:
Lisa Kuhn/Curio Press, LLC
www.curiopress.com

F+W PUBLICATIONS, INC.

This journal belongs to

_____

spring has sprung

To whoever might find this,
my name is Chris Lynch, and I'm pretty
sure I'm dying. In fact, if you are reading this,
then I'm probably already dead. Not that anyone
will be around to read this ... from what I've seen,
I'd guess this is the end of everything.

This is my poetry journal. In it, I will
attempt to capture the beauty I see
in the world in the form of a
poetic structure called "haiku." With three
simple lines composed of five syllables,
then seven syllables, and another line of
five syllables, I will attempt to capture
the earthly beauty which can be so
overwhelming that I sometimes feel
like I'm going to burst open. Enjoy.

I'm writing this from inside a locked bathroom
at the airport. After the plague, about a hundred
of us moved safely behind the fences of this
airport. For the past couple months,
we have been relatively safe here
because the dead

1

couldn't get past the fences. Well, then they figured out how to get past the fences. A girl named Barbara and I locked ourselves into an airport magazine shop. We lived off candy bars for a few weeks, and then let starvation run its course. Barbara died and turned into whatever the dead turn into,

The bird flew away
with more than just my bread crumbs.
He took my sorrow. •

If the dawn should break
and take away this sunrise,
I hope I break, too.

My soul hovers up,
climbing from its stomach cave,
to give my heart warmth.

which is why I had to attempt my suicide run for this bathroom. Somehow, people turn into these things when they die, or if one bites them. Long story short: I think I'm the only one left of our airport group, and it's not looking like I can hide out much longer. This journal that I'm writing in ... its former owner bit me. As I was trying to dodge my way through the crowd and into the safety of this bathroom, one of them grabbed me. I punched him. He bit me. I was able to get away and kill the guy (or re-kill the guy?) by slamming the bathroom door on his head, a lot. Not pretty. During the slam-fest, his arm got caught on this side of the door and I severed it off. In his hand was this journal.

If she calls tonight,
my heart will score one more point.
And doubt, minus one.

The woods are lovely.
They are dark and they are deep.
How I love the woods.

Fifty years from now,
When I am slow, old and gray,
will she be there, too?

Now I'm alone in a locked bathroom with a journal, a pen, and an arm of a dead man who came alive and died again. Is that murder? If so, lock me up. Ha Ha! I guess I'm already locked up, so case dismissed!

I can hear them out there, clawing at the door. I'm not going anywhere.

Chris L.

3

Dandelions

Joy! Magic exists!
An old dream of mine came true
and I think it's love.

Sometimes rain is sad,
but after the time we shared,
rain can't pull me down.

The tree in the wind
slowly bends like a dancer,
dancing in the sky.

Little mosquito,
where is it you have flown from?
Your name sounds Spanish.

My day starts off bad.
I'm running behind for work.
If I'm late, I'm dead.

Something on the news
about people acting odd,
so I switch to sports.

I grab a quick meal
while skimming through the paper.
Death, death, death, comics.

Dodging eye contact
from my neighbor's awkward stare,
I leave my nice house.

As I start my car,
my neighbor just keeps staring
and doesn't wave back.

Neighbor

Radio stations
are not playing any songs,
so I turn it off.

On the way to work,
I drive past lots of car wrecks
clogging up traffic.

A guy almost dies
stumbling onto the road.
Too drunk to walk straight.

Much to my surprise,
when I get to the office,
the place is empty.

When I call the boss,
he answers and screams at me
and then drops the phone.

Beth from accounting
is just sitting in her car
eating spaghetti.

Spaghetti?

I ask her what's up,
but she just eats in her car.
Something's wrong with Beth.

Odd that Beth won't speak.
Odder that Beth is eating
without utensils.

I tap on the glass.
Beth smashes her face through it.
I call 911.

I hit redial.
Another busy signal.
They need call waiting.

With glass in her neck,
Beth climbs out her car window
and reaches for me.

As I help her up,
and I know this sounds crazy,
Beth tries to bite me.

That stuff on Beth's face ...
there's one thing I know for sure:
that's not spaghetti.

We make quite the scene,
her moaning and me screaming,
but no one sees it.

Beth sort of hugs me,
which I am not a fan of,
so I kick and run.

I head for safety
to the nearby gas station ...
which is on fire!

People stagger out
from the burning gas station
as I run to help.

Alright, something's wrong.
These people look really sick,
and Beth's catching up.

Close-up

Strangers lunge for me
as the gas station explodes.
Maybe I'm dreaming.

I run to my car
and these people all follow,
but I'm done helping.

They surround the car
and are all moaning something.
Is that the word "trains"?!

I start the engine,
but it's really hard to steer
with Beth on my hood.

While I'm in reverse,
Beth starts punching my windshield,
then moves to head-butts.

I hit the ditch hard,
which is how my car got stuck
and how Beth got dead.

As I stumble out,
the sick people walk toward me
and I'm in trouble.

The only option
is a nearby billboard sign,
which I quickly climb.

My town is broken.
From this view, I see the end.
Below, they gather.

Below

They can't climb up here,
so they stand, moan and stare.
Somehow even Beth.

They don't talk to me.
Although I try to reason,
they don't seem to care.

As I scream for help,
my echo tricks those beneath
to stare for my twin.

My cell phone's no use.
Every number is busy,
which never happens.

For hours, I sit.
Morning turns to afternoon,
and they keep staring.

One guy beneath me
has his head twisted so wrong
that he should be dead.

Trouble

As day turns to night,
no one has come by to help,
so it's up to me.

creek ⤵

Starving and sunburnt,
it's time to get off this thing.
My plan: Jump and run.

The jump wasn't bad.
It's the running, however,
that didn't quite work.

Rolling in the grass
is not the best defense move
to escape large groups.

There was less punching—
this worst-case scenario—
and much more biting.

I am in trouble.
She is chewing on my neck
from ten feet away.

I managed to stand
and weave my way to the car,
but they keep biting.

I'm really torn up.
A hole in my neck whistles
with every inhale.

I'm now in my car,
most likely bleeding to death,
writing my last words.

My car

Anyone out there
reading this haiku journal,

give this to my mom.

Dear Mom, I love you.
This, ain't my most poetic,

but I really hurt.

Something is not right.
If my blood is in puddles,
why do I feel strong?

After I was bit,
I knew I was in trouble
when I bit me, too.

There's nothing quite like
the pain you feel while dying--
switching to hunger.

My skin is drying,
my veins are much more pronounced
and I'm turning gray.

The diseased outside
slowly stop clawing the car,
uninterested.

My lungs slow and stop,
and I can't find my heartbeat,

but I'm still hungry.

Although my neck hole
 used to whistle when I breathed,
now I don't breath.

I am so hungry,

and only one thing sounds good.
 Time to leave the car.

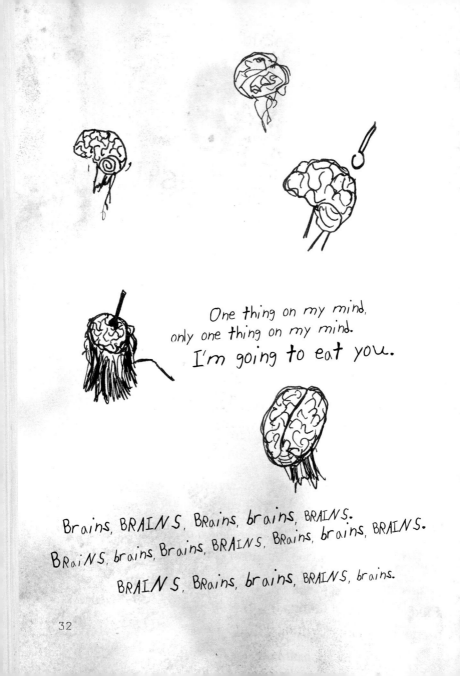

One thing on my mind,
only one thing on my mind.
I'm going to eat you.

Brains, BRAINS, BRains, brains, BRAINS.
BRaiNS, brains, Brains, BRAINS, Brains, brains, BRAINS.
BRAINS, BRains, brains, BRAINS, brains.

32

CRAWL

I exit the car
as the others slouch away,
off for fresher food.

As I start walking,
I try to remember where
people like to hide.

My memory slows,
and I can't remember much,
but I know enough.

34

I remember home,
and I remember my mom
and her meaty thighs.

I can remember
good food that Mom used to make.
I bet Mom tastes good.

Walking down the streets,
I just barely remember
how to find her house.

35

EYEBALL

Turning on her road
and seeing the porch light on
makes me salivate.

What is that low growl?
I look around and notice
that moaning is me.

Through the door's peephole,
    my mom just stands there and stares
as I claw the door.

The side porch window
lets us stare at each other,
both of **us yelling**.

I can't remember
how to open this window,
so I'll just stand here.

She won't let me in,
but I fix the window glitch
by leaning through it.

She is much faster,
but going upstairs leads nowhere,
and I'm much stronger.

Fresh food smells so good,
like pasta Mom used to make.
Mom's brains smell good.

I loved my momma.
I eat her with my mouth closed,
how she would want it.

My dad used to say,
"Always finish what you start,"
so I eat her hair.

I lose my front teeth
while trying to pry her hair
out from between them.

Thinking about Dad
makes me think of better times,
but then back to meat.

I bet Dad's upset.
He probably came back, too,
but coffins are dark.

Reanimation
would be much more difficult
inside a coffin.

SHINY LIQUID

Nothing left to eat,
    so I slowly leave Mom's house,
back out the window.

She's always with me,
especially if my gut
    can't digest toenails.

Through the neighborhood,
I try to remember where
people congregate.

My instinct steers me
to my gourmet dinner feast,
a nursing home.

The side door is shut.
From the side window, they stare.
So many meals stare.

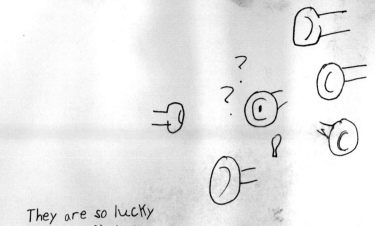

They are so lucky
that I cannot remember
how to use doorknobs.

I circle around,
and a great surprise greets me:
automatic doors.

REACH

46

It is hard to tell
who is food and who isn't
in the nursing home.

I really need blood.
Moaning "brains!" is hard to do
with a dried out tongue.

Little old ladies
speed away in their wheelchairs,
frightened meals on wheels.

Wheelchair pile-up!
Five old women on the ground,
helpless as babies.

Everything I thought

tasted a lot like chicken
really tastes like man.

Biting into heads
is much harder than it looks.
His skull is feisty.

TASTY NECK!

49

Teeth can bite through bones.
The hair is hard to swallow.

Brains squish easily.

You'd think I'd get full
eating so many people,
but ████ really, I don't.

My thumb poked something.
I think a lung just collapsed
because of the air.

He tends to not flinch,
though I'm yelling in his ear,
which is in my hand.

Looking at the hole,
can you hear without the ear,
or do you need this flap?

With a strong sucking,
they pop right into my mouth.

Eyeballs taste like grapes.

Due to my neck hole,
eating is more difficult.
Her toe popped back out.

In defense, he bites,
but my fingers don't feel pain.
Soon, neither will he.

Blood is really warm.
It's like drinking hot chocolate
but with more screaming.

It's time to move on.
Those moving aren't edible:

ones I ate too slow.

The fire alarm,
ringing as I leave the home,
calls no one tonight.

Walking in the dark
with a stomach full of meat,
I search for meat.

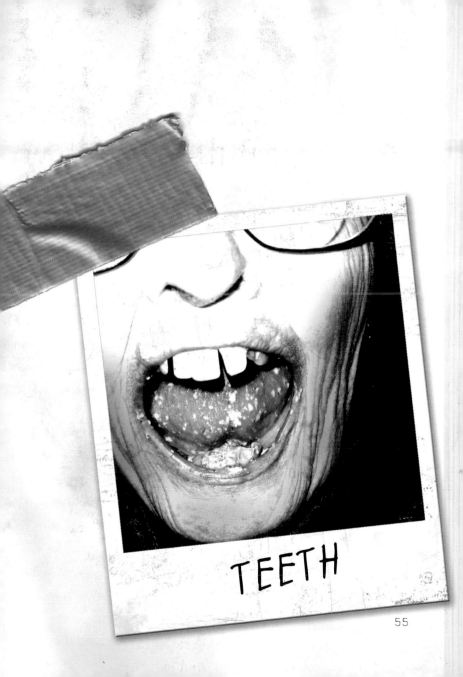

TEETH

Empty neighborhoods.
Except for a few like me,
nothing is moving.

Occasional screams
loudly tell me of missed meals
that others found first.

Highway entrance ramps
remind me of the city,
and my stomach growls.

There are lots of us
stumbling up the freeway,

all heading downtown.

We all think alike.
Thousands lived in the city,
thousands of fresh brains.

My shoes are slushy,
with my decomposing feet
leaking clear liquid.

HIGHWAY

My steps leave footprints.
Many of us leave a trail,
like snails on cement.

The slow walk takes days.
A speeding car hits a pole,
so we get a snack.

Others ahead moan
and soon we are all moaning:
The skyline in sight.

My nose is dripping.
The taste gets me excited,
seeping to my tongue.

Drumming above us,
a single helicopter
with nowhere to land.

The city smells ripe!
There are many of us there,
but alive ones, too.

A woman screaming,
as I walk off the highway,
begs me to help her.

She is still begging,
but no longer for my help.
She wants her nose back.

Many fall on her.
I stumble back and pick up
the stuff that falls out.

We fight over it.
He claws it out of my mouth
and puts it in his.

COMPETITION

Many are running.
The streets are clogged with thousands. Many are eating.

We mass together.
As people try to run past,
we just surround them.

We both start tugging.
He gets the hand and fingers,
but I get the arm.

The longer they're out,
    they turn wet red to dry gray,

        so I eat brains quick.

We all pile up,
falling over each other
    and the chubby boy.

There is something fun
about that soft popping sound
when biting fat calves.

64

Although we walk slow,
that dead-end alley, she chose
will speed up our meal.

Two of us take turns.
I chew when he bites and tears.
When I bite, he chews.

The flies on my neck
are starting to irritate
the other dead guy.

With his jaw snapped off,

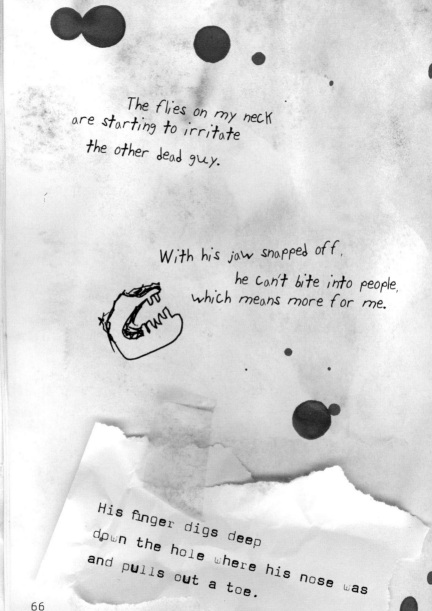

he can't bite into people,
which means more for me.

His finger digs deep
down the hole where his nose was
and pulls out a toe.

DEAD

I can see through you,
literally through your mouth
and out to the street.

The loud explosion
pulls our attention toward it
with hopes of fried food.

We all stand and wait
for the bus to stop burning
before we can eat.

Falling with the group,
by the time I get to her,
all that's left is hair.

Always be careful
when you're biting teeth with teeth.
Dead teeth tend to lose.

I push with my chin,
a better biting angle,
into her shoulder.

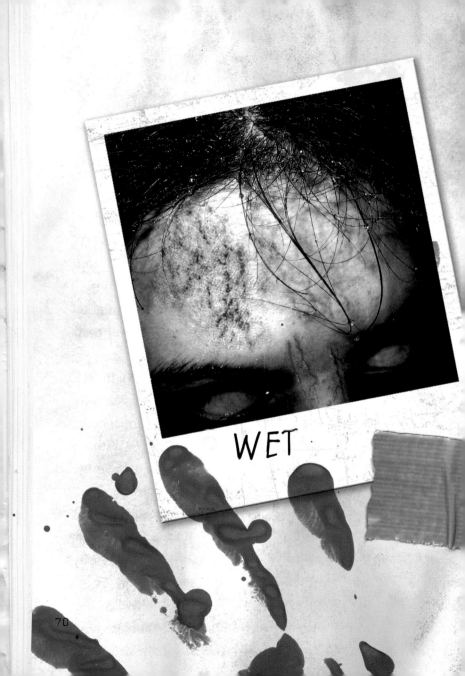

WET

Bones are hard to break.
The skull is not like an egg,
takes more whacks to crack.

One that gets away,
a man with a cricket bat,
cracks me in the face.

Buildings are burning
and ash covers everything.
Now they are gray, too.

Brains are less squishy
and a tad bit more squeaky
than someone might guess.

71

All I think about
is how hungry I will be
once I eat this foot.

Elbows bend one way,
except for this guy screaming.
His bends two ways now.

None of us walk well.
We bump into each other
as we chase the girl.

I trip in the mob
and get trampled for hours,
biting at ankles.

Getting trampled on
used to eventually kill you.

Now, it just annoys.

PULLING

Lying on the road,
a few ate until they burst.
I eat what burst out.

A man starts yelling

"When there's no more room in Hell...,"
but then we eat him.

All of us searching,
all of us with fat stomachs,
still frantic for more.

The city is dead.
Streets are just filled with people
who aren't quite people.

Food is running out.
Thousands rage with hunger pains.
No one's left to eat.

I lap around blocks.
The city, an empty plate,
has been licked clean.

Our group slowly thins.
One by one, we slip away,
off looking elsewhere.

Nothing left but bones.
Blood stains each building corner,
which some of us lick.

Down the empty streets,
my gurgles echo off walls
to which I moan back.

Looking at my hand,
somehow I lost a finger
and gained some maggots.

With nothing to eat
while passing the highway ramp,
I leave the city.

For miles, I walk.
Day turns to night turns to day.
So hungry, I walk.

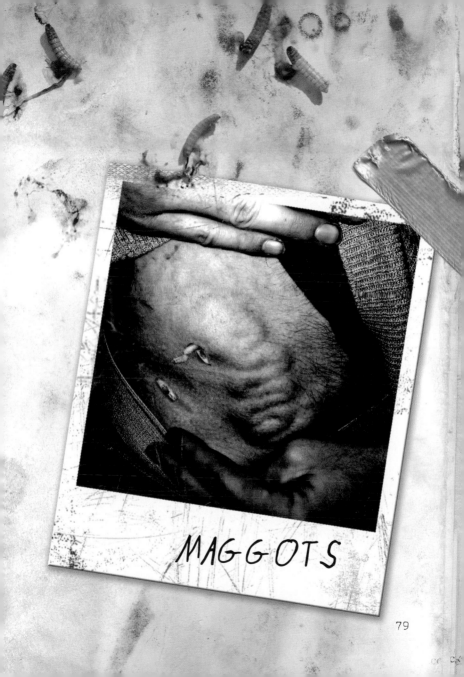

MAGGOTS

I moan to myself
on a deserted highway
under the moonlight.

At dawn, I see them

massed in a mall parking lot:
ones hungry like me.

The mall is empty.
What seems like was once a feast
is now just the dead.

I move from the mall
through parking lots and suburbs
to fields of nothing.

Walking across fields
is hard when you can't bend well.
Takes a lot longer.

Across a cornfield,
I find something exciting:
a house, surrounded.

The doors and windows
are covered shut with scrap wood,
but we can smell them.

Through a window crack,
my hand flails for one of them,
but they have hammers.

A rifle barrel
slides out from that window hole
and aims for our heads.

GIRL

Bodies pile up.
It seems bullets can stop us,

not that it stops us.

I smell in the air,

as we all lean on the door,
meat somewhere else, close.

Staggering away,
I follow the smell of brains
back into the fields.

Smelling the same meal,
another one of us joins me
into the darkness.

The other dead guy
stares at me with a blank look
as we softly moan.

I can see his tongue
move through the hole on his face
that isn't his mouth.

FIELD

We both lunge faster
as a distant barking dog
is told, "Be quiet!"

The other guy screams
as we lurch through the wheat field
and head toward the voice.

My strong sense of smell
helps wheat-field navigation
to a farmhouse porch.

Barking and screaming.
If I could still salivate,
my tongue would be soaked.

The porch door explodes.
A large man with a shotgun
          blasts my friend's leg off.

The screen door rips down
     and smashes on top of him
               as I lean though it.

He tries to stop me
by shooting me in the chest,
but that doesn't work.

Shotguns don't scare me,
which explains why I chased him,
and why I'm one-eared.

He runs down the steps,
which I am slow at going down,
but there's no way out.

Tripping down the steps
doesn't hurt me like it did,
but it's more often.

He turns off the light
and thinks he can hide from me,
but my nose finds him.

After his shovel
is slammed down into my face,
my jaw closes wrong.

BASEMENT

His dog bites my leg,
and he bites my shoulder blade
as I bite his head.

Nothing hurts me now.
Normally, the screwdriver
wouldn't have gone there.

What seems like an axe
is slammed into my ankle
as I bite his hip.

91

He keeps hitting me
even after I bite him,
but not much longer.

I know he can't see
because the room is pitch black
and I have his eyes.

His stuck fingernail
is lodged between my molars
and makes my mouth itch.

FRIEND

With more noise upstairs,
he becomes not my main course,

but appetizer.

My right foot snapped off
so I now walk on a nub.
Thus causing the lean.

Going up steps is hard
because of my missing foot
and a pissed-off dog.

She's in the kitchen,
scared and screaming her lungs out—
which I will soon see.

When I bend my knees,
  they creak like a rusty door,

    giving me away.

My right eye is stuck,
which is why I bend my head
while running at her.

My right arm won't bend,
which is why I can't hold her
  and she slips away.

My fingernail snaps,
ripping off on that light switch.

Now I'm down to six.

As she heads upstairs,
I work on the dog problem
with a microwave.

STEPS

The microwave falls,
and then I drop it again.
No more dog problem.

Upstairs is quiet.

But then one starts screaming,
quickly joined by more.

The crying baby
reminds me of fast food meals
with a prize inside.

Luckily I tripped--
or I would not have seen her
underneath her desk.

Her toes are like grapes
with the same rush of flavor.
Same juices, same pop.

Her tongue can't form words,
although it's still wiggling
when it's in my hand.

Falling down the stairs
wasn't too bad or painful.
Took a lot less time.

Two motionless boys
stare as I try to stand up
in the dark hallway.

The kids run from me
and dart outside through the door.
Not a good idea.

WHEAT

Stumble through the yard,
only to fall down and on
the guy with one leg.

Two are hard to hold.
One gets loose and one doesn't.
One for one-leg-guy.

The one I follow
escapes by climbing a tree
into a treehouse.

Finished with his meal,
one-leg-guy slithers over

and stares up with me.

One-leg-guy's last meal
was not completely eaten.
Now, three of us stare.

The boy in the tree
yells to his brother for help.
He moans in reply.

Not sure how to climb,
we all stare at the treehouse
and hope he comes down.

A few days go by
before he starts smelling bad
and becomes like us.

As I trip away,
he falls out of the treehouse
on his dead brother.

They claw at the ground,
pushing off of each other,
unable to stand.

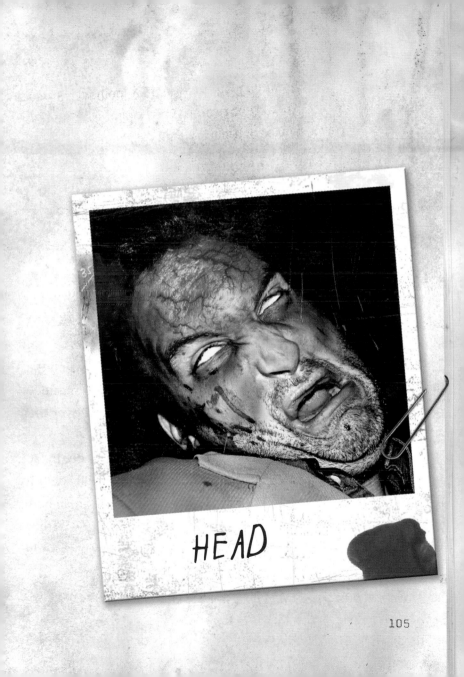

HEAD

The pile yells at me
because of my advantage.
I can walk, Kind of.

Alone through the fog,
I continue on my search
leaving them to wail.

It takes much longer
to cross a wheat field at night
walking on a stub.

In the woods at night,
tree branches rip through my skin,
but nothing leaks out.

I roam the forest,
hobbling for days and nights,
with no one to eat.

My body is weak.
Sometimes I stand in the woods,
not moving for days.

Skin bubbling up.
How did the maggots get there?
Now I'm all itchy.

I crawl more at night,
and during the day, I sit,
hoping to smell meat.

WOODS

A protruding bone
Keeps snagging on tree branches,
so I snap it off.

The flies on my arm

clearly have something to do
with all these maggots.

One eyeball has shrunk.
I'm glad it's tied to something
so it won't fall far.

My newest habit
is chewing on my forearms,
which slows the crawling.

I don't know how long
I was lying in the creek,
before I smelled them.

I somehow stand up.
I somehow start walking fast.

I smell lots of brains!

The scent is so strong,
if my stomach could still growl,
they'd hear me coming.

111

The odor leads me
to a clearing in the woods
where I hear more moans.

As I cross the field,
I see two others like me
watching children play.

We stand at the fence,
moaning as they play hopscotch,
too far from our reach.

FENCE

On the other side,
safely fenced in and secure,

sits a small airport.

For the next few days,
we watch groups of what we were,

living how we lived.

There's a lot of them.
Enough for us to eat well,
and then keep eating.

Through the large windows,
most of them stay inside
and rarely look out.

When some step outside,
the air becomes heavier,
and we bite the fence.

We push and we howl,
but they never come near us,
even though we beg.

More people like us
slowly come from all around
for people like them.

Days become shorter,
and it didn't used to snow,
as we stand and watch.

Our group keeps growing.
There are more of us than them,
all pushing the fence.

They throw gasoline,
and it splashes through the fence.
Then they throw a match.

Many of us burn,
which means I'll get to eat more
once we make it through.

I keep saying "brains."
I remember other words,
but I just need one.

A small group of them
climbs into a small airplane,
and it starts to move.

We watch it go up.

We watch it twist and dovetail.

We watch it go down.

We can't move the fence,
but a small plane exploding
sure knocks down a lot.

NO FENCE

The bent fence buckles
as hundreds lean and tumble.
We fill the runway.

A few run at us
wielding shovels and hammers,
which we take from them.

FELL

Rotten flesh tearing,
as the hammer rips my cheek,
hardly makes a sound.

Most run back inside
as some light a fire ring
around the building.

Fire, normally,
would stop us dead in our tracks,
but we're all hungry.

Being on fire
seems to not hurt me as much
as it's hurting him.

Intestines dangle.
As he crawls, they trail behind
from where I bit him.

His jaw in my hand
snapped easily off his mouth
and then into mine.

He is screaming words,
but I don't understand him
since I have his tongue.

Swallowing is hard.
My smile reaches my ear.
Food pops out the side.

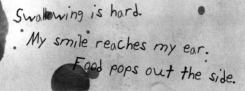

Although my teeth helped,
I'm surprised how well I chew
through heads with my gums.

I'm a slow eater.
The others finished their meals
and moan for seconds.

My rigor mortis
is mainly why I'm slower,

and the severed foot.

Through the giant glass,
we stare at them staring back
as the window bends.

SMILE

The glass wall stops us
until our weight together
helps us reach through it.

An alarm goes off

as we pile past the shards
and start grabbing meat.

The fat one I grabbed
fell as I ripped his stomach,
and burst on the floor.

Without their faces,
they still try to talk to me

until their throats rip.

We all fight for one
and climb over each other,
each taking a limb.

When too many heads
all try to chew on one head,
the lips don't last long.

It might be water,
from the cut between my toes,

dripping on his shirt.

Due to the carpet,
the lone discarded kneecap
is covered with hair.

She tugs at my face,
and somehow gets my eyeball
stuck on her necklace.

FACE

Brains, brains, brains, brains, brains!
Brains, brains, brains, brains, brains, brains, brains, brains!
Artificial hip?

We fall down the steps.
His neck snaps and he lays still.

Mine snaps, but I eat.

I need to slow down.
It's hard, when eating fingers,
to tell whose hand's whose.

The taste of liver
is hard to get off your tongue,
but spleen does the trick.

Small huddles of us,
eating in our frenzied packs,
dot the terminal.

It's over too fast.
I hunger longing for more
while I'm still eating.

AIRPORT

A man and a woman
run in a magazine shop
and pull down the gate.

We eat all the meat
until the only two left
watch us from their store.

Hundreds of us wait.
Many stand along the gate.
Some wait in the seats.

We watch them for days
as they live off the candy
and read magazines.

135

They are getting weak.
They yell at themselves and us.
All they do is cry.

We reach in their cage,
some pushing their elbows through,
and we beg for them.

Soon, they'll have to choose.
They're out of food and starving.
Die in there, or run.

Looks like they'll try both.
The girl dies but starts moving
as he leaves the shop.

Surprised he came out,
most pause as he runs by them,
but not me: I'm smart.

Well, it won't be much
longer NOW. All my limbs and joints
are tightening and it's getting hard for me
to write with this PEN. Suicide isn't
an option because I'll just come back faster.
The only way I can REALLY DIE
and not come back is if I can somehow
CUT off my HEAD, which isn't
too feasible in this bathroom.
Maybe I should just UNLOCK the door
and let them finish me.

I don't want to die.
If you are READING this, please find my wife

and tell her I loved her. Tell her

I'm SORRY for all the trouble
I caused in our MARRIAGE, and that SHE was

a great wife....

Tell her I LOVED her
and THAT I want TO EAT HER
AND SWALLOW HER BRAINS!

About the Author

It is believed that the above photo depicts Ryan Mecum, author of Zombie Haiku. Before the plague, he worked as a youth pastor at a Presbyterian church in Cincinnati, Ohio. In his spare time, he wrote poetry. Zombie Haiku was his first published work.

To George Romero:
Because of you, I'm screwed up.
Thanks for your movies.